MW00831912

Jesse Chisholm

Bust of Jesse Chisholm, located in Cherokee Museum, Cherokee, Oklahoma.

Jesse Chisholm

The story of
a trailblazer and peacemaker
in early Texas and Oklahoma

With best regards
Sybil O'Rear

by Sybil Jarnagin O'Rear

EAKIN PRESS ★ Austin, Texas

Published in the United States of America
By Eakin Press
An Imprint of Sunbelt Media, Inc.
P. O. Drawer 90159 ★ Austin, TX 78709-0159

2   3   4   5   6   7   8   9

ISBN 1-57168-110-8

Library of Congress Cataloging-in-Publication Data

O'Rear, Sybil J.
    Jesse Chisholm: the story of a trailblazer and peacemaker in early Texas and Oklahoma / by Sybil Jarnagin O'Rear.
        p.   cm.
    Includes bibliographical references (p.   ).
    Summary: Presents the life story of the part-Cherokee trailblazer whose greatest accomplishment was bringing the Plains Indians to the peace table.
    ISBN 1-57168-110-8
    1. Chisholm, Jesse--Juvenile literature. Pioneers--Texas--Biography--Juvenile literature. 3. Pioneers--Oklahoma--Biography--Juvenile Literature. 4. Cherokee Indians--Mixed descent--Biography--Juvenile literature. 5. Frontier and pioneer life--Texas--Juvenile literature. 6. Frontier and pioneer life--Oklahoma--Juvenile literature. 7. Texas--History--To 1846--Juvenile literature 8. Oklahoma--History--Juvenile literature.
    [1. Chisholm, Jesse. 2. Pioneers. 3. Frontier and pioneer life. 4. Texas--History. 5. Oklahoma--History.]   I. Title.
    F390.c45074   1996
    976.4'05'092--dc20
    [B]   96-24039
                                                                  Cip
                                                                   AC

Contents

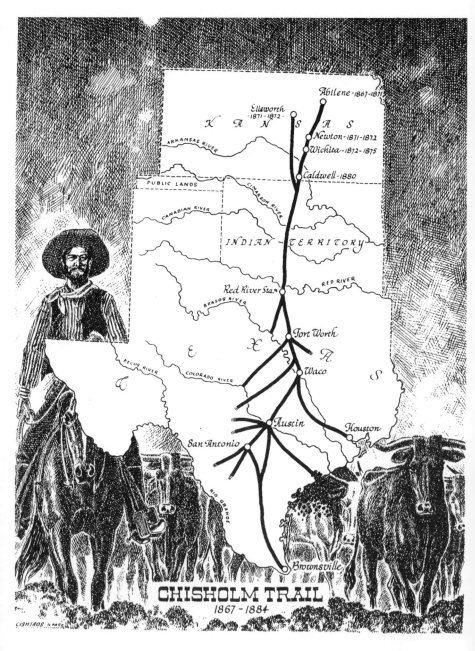

— Courtesy the artist, José Cisneros

Author's Note

When I taught Texas history all those years, I only knew Jesse Chisholm as the man for whom a cattle trail was named in the late 1860s. Thinking he was just another cattleman, I was surprised to find in my research that he was a very complicated person who lived between two worlds: white and Cherokee. Both his mother and his father were part-Cherokee, part-white.

Jesse lived most of his life with Cherokees, but sometimes with Creeks or other tribes. It is said that he was adopted by twelve different tribes and could speak fourteen different dialects, as well as English and some French and Spanish. With this language ability, it was natural for him to become an interpreter and peacemaker in troubled times.

The man loved nature, studying it from the

time he was a child, and developing a "homing instinct," which led to his becoming a trailblazer, guide, and good road mapper. He traveled widely, trading and trapping furs as he went, and he became a very successful merchant (peddler, really). This business kept him away from home much of the time, but his heart was so big, he eventually adopted thirteen needy kids to join the three of his own.

His generosity was extended not only to children but everyone who needed food, clothing, shelter, or counseling. It was often said about him, "No one ever left his home cold or hungry." However, his greatest achievement probably was in bringing the Plains Indians to the peace table with whites. He was, indeed, a very great man who made many friends with both common and important people of both races.

Since I could find no juvenile stories dealing with Jesse Chisholm, and very few amusing incidents in the two adult biographies about him, I was forced to create conversations and use other fictional approaches to make the story come to life. But I have tried to stay close to the truth at all times.

My friends Ovon Ross Booth and Howard Blasingame were generous and helpful in critiquing this manuscript; I'd like to thank them for this invaluable service. I'd also like to thank the Pasadena Public Library for obtaining several books through the Inter-Library Loan. I'd be remiss if I didn't thank Mary Chiltoskey of Cherokee, North Carolina. A retired teacher and writer, she went to the Cherokees many years ago, married a noted woodcarver named Goingback Chiltoskey, and stayed on to help preserve the original Cherokee culture. At my request, she sent information, newspapers, and other materials, which gave me a good start on research.

The afterword about the Eastern Cherokees was written after I had spent some time in the beautiful Smoky Mountain area of North Carolina and Georgia, where today's Eastern Cherokees live. Since both Jesse Chisholm and Sequoyah and their families originated in the East, I thought it fitting to add the material. During my stay there, I was pleased to attend an enjoyable and informative seminar that was taught by George Ellison, an area lecturer, writer, and naturalist.

I hope that you find this biography fun and instructive.

Jesse Chisholm

1

Cherokee Beginnings

Jesse Chisholm was thinking hard. He had so many questions about himself.

"Mamma, am I white or Indian?" he asked his mother.

"You are part Cherokee Indian and part Scottish. Your daddy's father, John Chisholm, was from Scotland. His wife, your Grandmother Patsy, was Cherokee."

Because the Cherokee family line comes down through the mother, the boy's father was considered Cherokee. His mother was part Cherokee, too, for her father had come from Scotland and married a Cherokee maiden, his Grandmother Jeannie Dew.

"Did all the men from Scotland marry Cherokees?" he wondered.

His mother smiled and said, "Many of them did."

In the late 1700s, very few Scottish young ladies came to America. When the men came, they met only Indians at the trading posts. Of course, many of them married Indians and had families.

"So part of me is white and part Indian?"

"That's right."

Jesse thought that was very special. But he decided he'd be an Indian most of the time because his family lived with the Cherokees.

He didn't know much about his family. One day he decided to ask his father, Ignatius, some questions.

"Daddy, what happened to your daddy? You never talk about him."

Jesse's father told him about John Chisholm. The man had come with others to live with the Cherokees years before. He found the people friendly, smart, and peace-loving. After marrying a maiden named Patsy, he decided that all the Indians were being mistreated by the white pioneers.

"One day he decided to go see the 'Great White Father' about this problem," his father continued.

"Great White Father?" Jesse asked.

"The president of the United States. He received the Indians and John Chisholm and told them they could stay 'as long as the rivers flow and the grass grows.' But many lawmakers thought that your grandfather was trying to start an Indian war. He got very upset and went back to Scotland."

2

"You won't ever do that, will you, Daddy?"

"No, but we may have to move farther west again."

Jesse's family and neighbors had moved once before, but now the white settlers were wanting more of their land again. In fact, they wanted all the land of the Five Civilized Tribes — the Cherokees, Creeks, Chickasaws, Choctaws, and Seminoles. All these groups lived in the eastern part of the young United States.

With his playmates and relatives, Jesse often went walking in the Smoky Mountain forests near his home. He loved the green trees which shed so much moisture that the mountains looked smoky all the time. A cousin told Jesse that was what gave the mountains their name — perhaps that was true.

As the boys returned from the forest one day, Jesse's father came in to show them a beautiful copper medallion that he planned to put on a chain and wear around his neck.

"Where did you get that pretty piece of jewelry?" his wife Martha asked.

"That strange crippled man, Sequoyah, makes them. He is a blacksmith and an artist too. He draws good pictures of animals, fish, flowers, and even people. He had a lot of jewelry to sell."

"Will you have him make me a necklace, Daddy?" Jesse cried.

"When you are a little older," his father replied, knowing that Cherokee children didn't wear jewelry until they were grown.

"I'll be a man someday," Jesse hoped.

"Yes, you will. But in the meantime, you'd better go to your uncle's for your lessons," his mother advised.

"Yes, Mamma."

A Cherokee boy was taught by his mother's brother instead of his father. The mother was the head of the family. She looked after the home and garden while the father hunted, fished, and fought necessary wars. Boys were taught how to use blow guns to kill birds and bows and arrows and traps to kill larger animals. They were also taught to play games — the most important one being stickball, a very rough sort of skateless hockey game.

Since Jesse was thought to be a Cherokee, his uncles taught him most of these things. But he respected and looked up to his father too. One thing his father and uncles discovered about him was that he never got lost in the woods. No matter how hard they tried to fool him, he could always find his way home. They said he had a "homing instinct."

"It may be that you'll grow up to be a guide," one uncle told him.

Not long after Jesse's father bought the pretty medallion, an uncle decided he wanted one and that Jesse could go with him to see

Sequoyah. Neighbors told Jesse that because Sequoyah was crippled in childhood, he couldn't hunt with the other boys and his grandfather had taught him to be a blacksmith. He had taught himself to draw beautiful pictures.

After looking at several of the medallions on hand, the uncle decided to have an eagle sketched on a round copper medal. Then Sequoyah took out a big piece of tree bark and drew a little picture of Jesse's uncle and an eagle on it. This was to remind him what to make and for whom.

When they left the shop, Jesse asked his uncle, "Why didn't Sequoyah just write down your name and what you wanted?"

"He can't speak or write English, and there is no written Cherokee language."

"You and my mamma and daddy can write, can't you?"

"Yes, in English. All of us went to the missionaries' school."

Not all Cherokees had gone to these schools — Sequoyah had not. His father was a white trader who married a Cherokee maiden. The trader wanted to move back to the white city, but his wife would not leave her village. He left his family alone. Sequoyah was so angry about this that he refused to have anything to do with whites from then on, including mission schools run by whites.

Many Cherokees had two names. Since Sequoyah's father was named Guess or Guest, he used both names sometimes. He was a very smart man who was trying to create a Cherokee alphabet, and he spent much of his time doing so. His wife often fussed at him because he didn't tend his shop all the time. She called him lazy, as did many other people.

The uncle continued talking about Sequoyah. "I hear he's always trying to teach Cherokee children our customs, words, and history."

"How can he do that if he can't write?" Jesse asked.

"He does everything aloud. And he always signs his name in English — it's shorter."

It was true that Sequoyah always signed the back of each piece of jewelry. And he was constantly trying to get Indians to work together for things that they wanted and needed, like more hunting grounds.

The next morning, Jesse's mother waked him and said, "Jess, hurry on with your clothes. We are going to see your uncle, the chief, today."

"My good clothes?"

"No, your everyday clothes."

Martha knew that the chief would probably have the boys playing stickball and practicing their bows and arrows together.

Jesse loved to go to his uncle's house. He hoped lots of his friends would be there when Uncle Jolly taught him about the bow. It was hard to pull the string back as far as he wanted to. But he was getting better, and if a crowd were there, he wouldn't be the very worst one. He jumped into his clothes and grabbed his headband.

"Mamma, what will the ladies do while we are playing?"

"First, we'll go to the garden to help your aunt get vegetables for the meal. We might pick blackberries too," she said with a smile.

She knew that he loved blackberries very much, and that those at his uncle's were usually ripe earlier. He smiled and remarked, "I hope that Uncle says my aim with the bow is better."

"He probably will. Are you wearing your fastest running moccasins?"

"Yes."

"I hear there's a big new boy there. You'll need them for the races."

2

A Friendship
with Colonneh

When they arrived at the chief's house, Jesse's father went inside to talk with Chief Jolly while the children went to play ball. They saw a tall scrawny buckskin clad teenager sprawled under an oak tree. He was so busy reading that he didn't even notice them come up.

One of the youngsters called out, "Colonneh, come over and play stickball with us."

The big fellow closed his book, put it in his pocket, and answered, "I don't know how to play stickball, but I'll bet I can hit that target down there oftener than you can."

Just as Sam went into the house to get his musket, Jesse's father and Chief Jolly came out to supervise the boys' play.

The chief said, "Boys, Colonneh's name is Sam Houston. He thinks he wants to stay with us and become a Cherokee. If he does, we must teach him our ways. He is strong and fast, but his ways aren't ours. Don't be too easy on him, but help him to learn. He'll pick things up quickly, for he's a smart fellow. He just doesn't like to farm or work in a store."

"He's not part Cherokee like me?"

"No, he's white. Though his name is Sam, we'll call him Colonneh, which means Raven."

"Why is he here?" Jesse's father asked the chief.

"He's the middle boy in a big family. He says they all bossed him on the farm — that he could never do anything right. Then they sent him to work in a store in Maryville. He can't stand measuring cloth and weighing potatoes all day. I'll see how he works out here."

Just then, Sam came out of the house with his long musket. While the crowd watched, he hit the middle of the target. Then the Cherokee boys went one at a time with their bows and arrows. Each boy hit the target — even Jesse. But Colonneh was the only one who hit the bull's eye.

The chief said, "That's very good — all of you. Now let's see how fast you can shoot."

Each boy shot three times, as fast as he could draw back an arrow. All did fairly well each time, but although Sam hit the bull's eye, he took a long time to reload every time.

"Muskets are not as fast as arrows, are they?" Sam said.

"No, they are not. They are a lot louder too. If you really want to be a Cherokee, Colonneh, you must learn to use the bow," said the chief.

"I can learn. Just give me a little time."

"I have to get better too," Jesse said, and his father nodded.

"Now it's time for the foot races," the chief said.

All the boys got in a line, and at a signal from Jesse's father, the race began. Jesse ran as fast as his good moccasins would carry him, but he came in behind Colonneh and several older Cherokee boys.

Chief Jolly said, "Good, Colonneh, you beat them all. But could you do that all day long?"

"No, I don't think I could. I've never tried."

"When we hunt in the winter, sometimes we chase a deer all day."

"I'll take a good while to learn that too."

Jesse turned to his father and said, "I'll have to practice a lot too."

Ignatius, Jesse's father, commented, "That's true. But you're very young. You're only seven. Sam is a teenager. He'll learn, and so will you."

Jesse decided that he liked this big teenager named Sam Houston. If Sam lived at Chief Jolly's, maybe he could see him often.

Soon after that, Jesse went with his uncle back to see Sequoyah. They were pleased with the pretty new medallion — the etched crane's long legs and graceful neck were just right. Jesse kept looking at the carved animals while Sequoyah and his uncle spoke about "talking leaves," which were sheets of paper with writing on them. All the time they talked, Sequoyah was melting silver coins to make jewelry.

He heard the jeweler say, "Someday I may be able to put Cherokee words on leaves of paper, instead of pictures on bark. I saw a book and the writing doesn't look that hard."

"Yes, but don't you remember our story about the Great Father creating an Indian and a white man? He gave the Indian a bow and arrow and the white a book."

"I don't believe it," the lame man said. "You'll see."

Jesse decided he wanted one of the carved birds and began making plans to get it. Maybe he could get a raven. He thought it very strange that when he went back to see the chief, he found Colonneh carving a piece of wood.

"What are you making?" he asked.

"A duck, but I'm having trouble."

"Have you seen Sequoyah's carvings?"

"Not yet, but Chief Jolly says we'll go there soon. He needs some blacksmith work done."

"Sequoyah is a good blacksmith. He's also trying to write in Cherokee."

"I can read and write well in English, but I hate to go to school. I can't be still that long."

When they played the games another day, Jesse saw that Sam had really been working on his aim with the bow and arrow. It was much better. He admired this big boy, or should he say man, for Sam was bigger than most men. He hoped that he'd be that big someday — and he might.

By the day of the Green Corn Dance, Chief Jolly had adopted Colonneh, making him an official tribe member. Sam was wearing the traditional Cherokee tunic and turban. (Cherokees often dressed differently from other tribes.) Jesse, who had gone early with his ten-year-old Aunt Talahina (Tiana), thought Sam was the handsomest one there — and so did Tiana.

Working his way through the crowd to Sam's side, Jesse asked, "Colonneh, don't you ever get homesick for your family?"

"My father is dead. I miss my mother. She was always good to me, but my brothers shoved me around too much. Then they made me work in that awful store."

"I think it would be fun to work in a store and meet all those new people," Jesse said.

"But you don't have time to talk to anyone. You'd be weighing nails or measuring gingham all the time. I'd rather learn to kill a deer with my bow."

"Are you practicing much with it?"

"A good bit. Say, Jess, why don't you come practicing with me tomorrow? We both need to work on our bows."

Jesse was so pleased; he could hardly answer. But finally he mumbled, "I'll have to ask my mother and tell you after the games. Are you dancing with the others now?"

"No, today I just watch the festivities because I've not been a Cherokee long enough."

When the drums began, the dancers took their places and danced round and round, celebrating the new harvest of corn. Cherokee women were the farmers, but everyone danced in celebration of the new crop. Days before had been spent cleaning, throwing away old pots and baskets, and getting ready for a new start.

After dancing around the bonfire, the Cherokees welcomed their medicine men and story tellers, who related again the wonderful things in their past history. In deep and wonderful voices, the old men told of the world's creation and of the big role all the animals played in the beginning.

Jesse loved all the celebration, especially the stories. He hoped he'd dream about those things that night. If he borrowed his sister's "dreamcatcher," perhaps he could. She had explained to him that the big circle of net that she hung above her bed would catch the bad dreams and let the good ones go through the hole in the middle. She said this dreamcatcher really worked. Jesse wanted to try it out.

Sam had enjoyed the festivities, too, and when everything was over, he found Jesse to ask about the next day.

"What did your mother say about tomorrow?"

"She said I might go."

Not only did Sam go with Jesse that day, but many other times. He developed a liking for the younger boy, and he became a good teacher to him. Soon they were both showing better aim. One morning they both were thrilled when Sam killed his first deer with his bow.

"Do you think I'll be able to do this soon?" Jesse wanted to know.

"Your arms have to get a might stronger, Jess. But don't give up. You'll do it in a few months. Your aim is getting better. Eat a lot of food!"

"I'll try."

Chief Jolly helped Sam skin the deer and cut up the meat. Then he asked him, "What are you doing with the pelt?"

"I was going to give it to you."

"No, this pelt is your first one. It is yours."

3

War of 1812 Causes Changes

The next morning, Sam was up with the sun. He went immediately to see the chief, and said, "Chief Jolly, I want to go into Maryville to get some things."

The chief nodded his head, but wondered if Sam would remain with his family there. He did not ask the question. Perhaps the boy was not as happy with the Cherokees as he seemed. Jesse also wondered if Colonneh would return, for he remembered that the teenager missed his mother.

They need not have worried. What Sam wanted to do was to buy gifts for his many Indian friends. Maybe the deer skin would pay for all of them.

The store owner was surprised to see Sam after so many months. He got all the purchases together quickly, hoping one of the brothers would come in while the young fellow was there. They didn't show up before he left. The one little pelt barely paid for the scissors, cloth, thread, knives, beads, and hard candy Sam bought.

He said to the clerk, "I'll be back when I get more pelts for more presents."

Sam was very proud of these gifts — the very first ones he'd bought with money he had earned. When he worked in that store, all his money had gone to his big family's support. Now he had a different family and wanted to show them how thankful he was for what they were doing for him.

The walk to and from Maryville was not nearly so tiring as it had been before he'd practiced all summer. Sam realized that he might be able to run all day if he kept it up.

Upon returning, he told Jesse and the other boys all about the trip as he gave them small gifts. The big presents went to Chief Jolly and his family; they were the ones who were doing so much for him.

Since Sam was a good bit older than Jesse, and now much better with the bow, they were not together so much. Still, Jesse admired the older boy greatly and really hated to see him leave when his two brothers came for him. They said his mother was grieving too much over him. Colonneh didn't want to leave his Cherokee brothers, but he loved his mother, too, so he went.

The big teenager was so unhappy back on

16

the farm that his mother let him return to the Cherokees in less than a year. This time he stayed two years. Again he bought gifts for everybody — so many that he ran up a huge debt. He owed more than $100 at the store. That was a great amount of money for a teenager to owe back then. Jesse knew that Colonneh would pay back the debt when he could. Sam respected his little friend, too, but didn't realize how important Jesse would be to him later on. One day he'd depend on Jesse to make peace with many people.

Meanwhile, Jesse had learned all the games and was considered the real leader among his friends. He became the high scorer in the boys' stickball games, and the entire team helped him celebrate his first deer kill. His father helped him prepare the meat, and his mother made several pairs of pretty moccasins from the pelt. Now he was looking forward to his twelfth birthday so he could go through the Cherokee manhood rite. That was still several years away.

While Jesse was visiting his grandfather one day, his young Aunt Tiana said to him, "They tell me that your friend Colonneh got in debt at the Maryville store."

Jesse angrily replied, "I know Sam will pay the bill someday. He'll find a way to make the money."

And, of course, he was right. When Sam left the Cherokees, he went home and opened a school for the pioneer kids, at prices even higher than the going rate. The young man was so well-liked by everyone (except his brothers) that he had no trouble getting pupils to sign up for his classes. He did pay the store back.

Jesse's uncles took him with them often to hunt and sometimes just to walk in the beautiful forest. He learned how to find old hidden trails, to decide when water was near from the looks of the plants, and to find all kinds of berries, nuts, and fruit. His grandfather noticed that he was quite interested in trailblazing.

He said to the boy, "Grandson, this trail-blazing skill of yours is very valuable, but you need to work on languages too. If you know several, you'll be in great demand as a guide and peacemaker. You know we are having troubles with the Creek Indians and some other tribes. Part of it is because we don't understand each other. Someone needs to be a 'go-between'."

"Yes, Grandfather. My friends tell me Sequoyah is still working on our written language, and that he wants all tribes to work together."

"That is true. But Sequoyah is only interested in the Cherokee language. There are many more to learn. I hear that he's almost given up trying to make a symbol for each word. You know there are about 20,000 words in our language."

"That would be a big job."

"Yes, and his wife does not like him to spend all his evenings on those 'talking leaves' of his. "

It was quite true that Sequoyah was becoming discouraged with his language work. He had first tried thousands of symbols. He'd have to think of something else.

One day Jesse and a friend passed by a new cabin on their way to the deep forest. Wondering whose it was, and since the door was open, they walked in. Tree bark was all over the table, and polk berry juice and brown walnut coloring were in little pots near turkey feather quills. They decided it must be Sequoyah's cabin. Dust covered everything, and there was a huge pile of bark, reaching almost to the ceiling.

"He hasn't been here in a long time. Don't touch anything. Do you think he's ever coming back?" Jesse wondered.

"My mother told me that people think he's losing his mind. He's just about quit doing anything," the friend answered as they left.

Sequoyah was not the only one having problems. Pioneers were making more demands on the Indians' lands. And the new United States was about to get into another war. England, their former mother country, was causing trouble again. Both the United States and England had tried to get the Indians to help them. Though the Cherokees were usually peaceful, when their enemy the Creeks joined with England, the Cherokees sided with the United States. Jesse's father, Ignatius, being only part Cherokee, and being older than most braves, decided not to go to war. He would help care for the families of those who did go. The year was 1812, and it was a bad year.

One day Jesse's mother said to him, "They tell me that Sequoyah is going to war."

"How can he fight if he is lame?" Jesse asked.

"He hasn't always been lame. Once he was strong and straight. Many people remember how brave he was; they have talked the army leaders into taking him. He has real spirit and will be good for the younger ones."

It was not long before they heard that young Sam had also joined the army. Jesse knew that he'd be a good warrior and wished that he were old enough to fight. However, when he said this to his grandfather, he was told he should be glad he wasn't old enough, that he should try to be a peacemaker instead. Jesse wondered why his grandfather was always saying things like that. Maybe it was because he was old. Jesse was listening to the older man's advice about languages, though, and was learning several Cherokee dialects from neighbors.

Jesse was ten when the warriors came back home. They told the children about Sam Houston's being wounded but then fighting on until General Andrew Jackson stopped him. A Creek arrow hit Sam in his groin and English bullets wounded his arm and shoulder. The bad arrow wound would bother him the rest of his life. But Sam stayed on in the army to help the general, Andy Jackson.

Andy became a good friend and helped him into a hospital in New Orleans.

Sequoyah had not been wounded, but he showed great bravery in battle. His tribesmen again thought him courageous and smart, and forgot about his work with the bark pictures. But while Sequoyah was in the army, he had been very envious of the soldiers who got letters from home. Only English-speaking soldiers did that. He came back determined to continue his work on the Cherokee alphabet.

4

A New Home in Arkansas

Even while the War of 1812 was going on, the frontier Americans kept pushing westward and demanding more land from the Indians. Although the Cherokees were peaceful and quite civilized, with farms, good log houses, and domestic animals, this didn't stop the frontier demands. Sam Houston saw that all Indians were fighting a losing battle, and so did Ignatius Chisholm.

In 1815 Ignatius decided to move his family to northwestern Arkansas territory. He had heard that this area was like their Smoky Mountains, and that there were few whites there.

This was to be a great adventure for ten-year-old Jesse. He was already a seasoned woodsman whose uncles had taught him well. Now his father became the main teacher, for the first time. The two grew much closer together because of the absence of many playmates and some relatives. On their way west, his father taught him to watch for unmistakable landmarks, like unusual shaped hills and unique villages. Then, when they got out of the mountains, he was taught to notice the strange new plants, the different types of farms they passed, and the many new kinds of trees.

One day Jesse's father said, "Jess, you might want to go back this way someday. You'd better remember how to do it."

They sometimes traveled on land and sometimes on flatboats or rafts on the winding Tennessee River. Though Jesse had been in canoes on their small rivers and creeks back home, he'd never been on big boats before. He was really excited when they reached the Mississippi River. The boats and rafts were even larger, and the water was swift and unbelievably wide. Jesse and Talahina, who had come with them, never tired of watching people on boats they met or passed. He was glad she had come with them, for he was already missing his friends and neighbors from home.

The captain was a big friendly Irishman, and Jesse developed a liking for him right away. He watched the fellow steer the boat to a landing every time they took on passengers or cargo. The happy captain explained many things to his young passenger.

One day he told Jesse, "I hope we meet that big steamboat. I'd like for you to see it."

"Steamboat?"

"Yes. It's run by a huge side waterwheel that's turned by steam. Men don't have to row it, as we do. It puffs lots of black smoke from pipes on top — makes noise too! They say some boats have paddlewheels on the back, and others on the side like that one. The *New Orleans* is the only one I've seen."

"And nobody rows it?"

"No, the paddlewheel does that. Of course, men have to feed wood into the fire that heats the boiler for the steam that turns the wheel."

The captain pointed out landings that he thought would turn into cities someday. Only a few years later, one of these would become Memphis (Tennessee's largest city today).

When the group reached the Arkansas River, they left the Mississippi and traveled on the smaller river until they reached the hills of western Arkansas. Ignatius decided that this was enough like the Smokies to suit him. They were in Johnson County, now a part of the Ozark National Forest.

Martha, Jesse's mother, said, "This is very pretty land. I'm glad we're stopping here."

The new home was beautiful. Game was plentiful, and the land fertile enough for vegetable gardens. Jesse wondered why the steep little mountains weren't smoky like the ones at home, but he didn't ask questions like that these days. He enjoyed the hunts with his father, and was becoming a very good shot with both bow and arrow and gun. They hunted often, sometimes exchanging the pelts for supplies at the nearest store or trading post.

For two years, Jesse and his father roamed the new territory, learning where the creeks and occasional farms were. The boy learned to find streams by studying the leaves of plants and the paths of animals, which often led to water. His uncle's prediction that he'd become a guide was coming true. In this sparsely settled area, he had more freedom than he'd had back in the more settled East. And though he was friendly with both Indians and whites, he was beginning to enjoy being alone with nature.

One day he began wondering if he could find his way back to his former home and friends. He began testing himself. His father understood what he was doing and was not surprised when Jesse came to him and said, "Daddy, do you think I could find my way back to the Smoky Mountains?"

"Yes, I believe you could," his father replied. "You might get lost now and then, but I think you could find the way back."

"Will you help me convince Mamma that I can do it?"

"Yes, I'll talk to her soon."

So, in 1817, when Jesse was only twelve years old, he went from western Arkansas to the

Tennessee-North Carolina border — all alone and with very few supplies and no money. He would kill game along the way and exchange the pelts for supplies. He probably worked on boats going upstream — not on steamboats, though he probably saw one on his trip, for they were making regular runs by then.

He was able to go directly to his old home and to completely surprise his relatives.

When he arrived, he found that many things had changed in two years. Of course, he expected his cousins to have grown, and they had, just as he had. But it was the adults who seemed so different. Most of them were sad and worried. The white settlers had made many more claims on their hunting grounds, and even on their farms. These peaceful Cherokees were thinking warlike thoughts, and many of them were thinking of leaving.

Jesse got a really warm welcome from his Grandfather Rogers, who gave a big dinner in his honor. Most of the family seemed surprised that he had been able to find his way back, but not his grandfather, who said, "I have always known that Jess would be a guide and trailblazer. He studies nature all the time."

Then the group began discussing Sequoyah, the lame blacksmith. He had gone to see officials with the nearly finished Cherokee alphabet. He had hoped to get tribal help in setting up a school so that the children could learn to write their Cherokee language.

Many tribal members had now decided that Sequoyah wasn't crazy after all. For years they had wondered about him. He'd built a cabin deeper in the woods, where he and his little daughter stayed most of the time. Now it seemed that he had actually captured the sounds made by the people speaking the Cherokee language, and had almost finished setting it down in what he called a syllabary (alphabet).

"Grandfather, what do you hear about Sam Houston?" Jesse asked.

"They say that he's still in the army, but acts as an agent to all Indians now. He may come to see us soon."

"I hope he comes while I'm here. I'd really like to see Colonneh."

And so it happened that in a few days Sam did walk up to the Rogers home. He saw Jesse and called out, "Hello there, Jesse! You've grown a foot since I last saw you!"

"Not quite — maybe half a foot. We've moved away, and I'm visiting my grandfather."

"That's what I hear. How'd you get back?"

"By boat and foot."

"Did your father come with you?"

"No, I came alone."

"You've really become a man then."

"Perhaps. Welcome back, Colonneh. Will you be here long?"

"No, I'm acting as agent now, and need to talk with the Cherokees. When I finish, I'll return to the army. General Andy Jackson has told me that I should study law and go into politics. I'm thinking about that."

Jesse went with the entire village to hear Sam speak. The man was still a true friend of the Indians, but because he knew what was going to happen, he advised them to sell their lands. They should move west where they could find more hunting grounds and farm lands, he said. Sam was very kind, but told them in no uncertain way that the whites would take their land if they didn't leave now. He made them admit their difficulties and their small numbers compared to the white frontiersmen.

Jesse watched his idol win the support of many of his tribesmen, including his own Grandfather Rogers. He would never forget Colonneh's exciting speeches and his valiant attempts to bring peace to both sides. Later in life, Jesse would do the same thing many times.

In the War of 1812, the Cherokees had helped the United States win the Battle of Horseshoe Bend against the Creeks and England. Because of their help the Cherokees had expected the young country to give them more respect, and not to keep pushing them out of their hunting grounds. But they were wrong. It seemed that Andy Jackson, who was later elected president, forgot all about their help. He hated Indians. To him, the Indian had land needed by frontiersmen like himself.

Sam Houston, though a friend of Jackson, saw what was happening to the Indians. He hated to tell the Cherokees that they should leave their beautiful mountains, but he knew they must.

That afternoon, Jesse's grandfather said to Jesse, "You know Colonneh is right, Jess. I have decided to follow his advice. I can get a good price for my holdings now."

"Yes, Grandfather."

"Jess, I have been watching you throughout all these talks. You've become a man. I thought so when you found your way back; now I know so. Do you think there's plenty of land where your father is?"

"Yes, I think so. He and I walk through lots of vacant land often."

"And do you think you could guide me and my group back to it?"

"Yes, I think so."

Jesse was very pleased that his grandfather thought him a man. First Sam Houston had said so, and now his grandfather. His mother would be happy to have more relatives near her. This was very good.

Captain Rogers was not a poor Cherokee but an educated and wealthy land owner and merchant. He was also an important political person in tribal affairs; many tribesmen would be influenced by what he did.

It took several weeks for them to sell the land and decide what to take with them. Finally, they got their possessions down to three wagon loads. Jesse led them to Knoxville, where they boarded flatboats on the Tennessee River. When they reached the Mississippi, they traveled down it to the Arkansas, just as his father had done before. Then the Arkansas took them to the Dardenelle settlement, where they spent a week before going on to the Chisholms' land.

It had taken them three months to make the trip. Jesse was proud of this accomplishment, but he didn't brag about it. That would have been unlike a Cherokee.

Martha Chisholm was overjoyed to see her son bring in her father's family. But she had sad news to give them. Her husband, Ignatius, had gone hunting weeks ago, and though he had intended to return in a few days, he had not. She was afraid something had happened to him.

5

The Search
Leads to a New Career

Captain Rogers was overjoyed to see his daughter and to tell her what a fine job Jesse had done in bringing them west. Not once had he lost his way. Then he rewarded his grandson by giving him a very good hunting knife. This was something all Cherokees valued greatly.

After the welcoming festivities, Jesse and his mother helped the group get settled in their new homes. He and his mother tried to persuade each other that Ignatius Chisholm would soon return, but as time wore on, they gave up hope. It had been such a long time since he left.

One day Jesse said, "Daddy must have had an accident in one of those trading towns. I must go to find him."

Martha Chisholm answered, "Yes, my son. But be very careful. I don't want something to happen to you too."

Jesse and his father had often been told that there was an unusual place south of them named Hot Springs. Since he knew his father wanted to go there, the boy decided that this would be a good place to begin the search.

When he got there, Jesse found that it was just as pretty as he had heard. There were three nice lakes and more than forty springs around the base of a small mountain. Indians of several tribes were bathing in the springs. Jesse, who could speak to some of them, learned that the hot springs helped cure many diseases and pains. However, none of the people had seen or heard of a man named Ignatius Chisholm. Some of them suggested that he try at Little Rock, for that was a big trading post.

At Little Rock, some fifty miles to the east, Jesse ran into the Arkansas River again. This trading town on the banks of the river had been begun by Frenchmen many years before. They called it *Petite Roche,* meaning little rock, because it was on a bluff over the river. There was a higher and larger bluff nearby.

Jesse found out that the French explorers and traders had been all over the territory. They had named many streams and had put trading posts everywhere. They had also left some of their customs and foods. Many of the trading posts were named for the Chouteau brothers, whose headquarters were said to be in St. Louis (a good way up the Mississippi River).

Getting no news of his father in Little Rock, Jesse went on until he reached the Mississippi. Then he went south, visiting Vicksburg and Natchez, Mississippi. In these places, he heard the French language again, as he had done in Little Rock. Since this language interested him, he tried to learn a few words. He did not know that the entire area once belonged to France.

He continued southward until he reached the city of New Orleans, Louisiana. Its size surprised him and he had some trouble adjusting. French was spoken here, but also Italian, English, and other languages, for this was a city more European than American. (Even today this is true.) At the busy docks, men were loading goods on ocean-going vessels. Jesse dreamed about the places they might be going to. He had discovered that he really liked to travel.

Nobody had heard of or seen his father; Jesse made sure of this before he started back home. He decided to get away from the river on his way back and go through central Louisiana.

At the small town of Marksville, he went to various places with his usual questions, but had no success. Then the sounds of a blacksmith shop interested him as he was leaving town. Thinking of his friend Sequoyah, he stopped to look in at the open door. A tall, jolly man was talking to the smithy, telling him all about a fight he'd had the day before. He seemed to be waiting for a knife to be finished. When the man saw Jesse, he walked over and said, "My name is Jim Bowie. What's yours, son?"

"Jesse Chisholm."

"Did you see that good knife the smithy is working on? It's made from my brother's plan — a dandy one! Do you have a knife, Jesse?"

"Yes, sir," he answered, unsheathing his new knife.

"Where did you get this knife, Jesse?"

"My grandfather gave it to me."

"That's a very good piece of steel. Your grandfather is a good judge of knives. You don't live around here, do you, son?"

"No, in Arkansas. I'm looking for my father, who disappeared on a hunting trip some time ago."

"Where have you been?"

"To New Orleans."

"Well, I haven't seen any strangers around here, have you, Smithy?"

The smithy shook his head, and Jesse left. He didn't know that he'd just met a man who would make his way into Texas history three times: once as owner and user of the famous Bowie knife, then as a searcher of the Lost Mines at San Saba, and finally as one of the commanders of the Alamo. Jesse would meet Bowie later, when he traveled to Fort Smith, Arkansas, to sell some slaves.

Jesse traveled on through Louisiana's plantation country and logging settlements, then into Arkansas, and on home. Not a single person had seen or heard of Ignatius Chisholm in all the places he had visited.

It was a very tired and saddened boy who arrived at his mother's. Martha had not heard anything encouraging. Jesse became so restless that he again left to search for his father, after only a few days at home.

This time he decided to go east. Perhaps his father had gone that way and then got the idea of going back to the Tennessee country to see how the other Cherokees were doing. He loved those Smoky Mountains. And he may have found trouble on the way.

About halfway to the Smokies, Jesse was surprised to run across a group of people who turned out to be Cherokees. There were almost 300 of them, headed in the wrong direction if they thought they were going to Arkansas, as one of them said. At the back of the group was Chief Jolly!

His old uncle was overjoyed to see him, and said, "Jess, what are you doing way over here?"

Wondering why they were going east, Jesse answered him, "I'm really looking for Daddy. He has been gone too long on a hunt. I thought he might have come back to the old home."

"We haven't seen him. Where was he going?"

"We don't know. I've been many places looking. But where are you people going?"

"We hope to get to the Arkansas."

"I'll go back with you," Jesse said, realizing that they were lost and needed someone to guide them.

When they reached the Mississippi, feeling sure that they could now go on safely, Jesse took his leave. He'd go to St. Louis this time. If that was such a big trading center and the home of the famous Chouteaus, he'd like to see it anyway.

St. Louis was quite different from New Orleans. It was smaller and friendlier. Again he found Frenchmen, but they were different from those in the bigger city. They were happy, country people who were traders and frontiersmen. They laughed and joked with each other all the time. Even though Jesse couldn't understand their language, he realized it was not the same French he'd heard before. And these people talked with their hands, their black eyes, their whole bodies. They were fun to watch, and again he found himself trying to learn a new language.

He found the Chouteau Company soon and had no trouble getting a job loading huge stacks of animal skins on boats. Indians brought these in constantly. Jesse, who was now fourteen and strong as a man, was a good worker on the docks.

After a hard day's work, the dock workers would gather at someone's house, or even in the streets, for food, music, and dancing. Accordion and fiddle players preformed energetically to keep up with the fast dancing. At first, Jesse sat on the sidelines watching, but he couldn't keep his feet still — they kept tapping away. And before the night was through, he'd decided he must learn this lively dancing; it was so different from that of the Cherokees.

Although all the workers danced until late in the night, they were up early, working as if they'd had a good night's sleep. It took Jesse a long time to learn to do this and to eat their spicy food.

As Jesse worked with the jolly Frenchmen, he began realizing something he hadn't noticed before. Though he was part Cherokee, he looked white, and because he did, he was accepted by whites wherever he went. Had he looked like an Indian, he would not have been accepted. He saw that a majority of whites in the business world looked down upon the Indians, and treated them unfairly. Neither did the Indians fully accept the whites. They thought white men were wasteful, foolish, and dishonest.

Jesse saw how little the merchants paid the Indians for their pelts, and then how much they got for their shipments. There was much money to be made in this trading business, even if the Indians were paid more.

Jesse knew where he could get the pelts. He decided he would open trading posts, and treat the Indians fairly. But he would still make a fortune, just as the Chouteaus had done.

6

Expert Guide and Trader

Martha Chisholm and Jesse lived a fairly peaceful life for several years. Tiana was often with them because she helped her sister, Martha, when she "kept boarders," as she often did to make ends meet. Jesse helped by using the trading lessons he had learned in St. Louis. He roamed all over western Arkansas, and what is now eastern Oklahoma, in hunting the plentiful game. Then he would usually sell his pelts in Fort Smith, where Indians came to trade, and where soldiers were stationed after 1817. They gave him good prices.

In 1820 the Cherokee agent to western Arkansas, Matthew Lyons, came to board at the Chisholm home. He became one of Jesse's idols. This old man had been through the Revolutionary War, had been in Congress, and was a friend of Andy Jackson (who got Matthew appointed). His stories were very interesting and he loved to tell them to Jesse. The two impressed each other. Jesse's trips into the wilderness and his growing knowledge of languages and people were bringing him respect from everybody he met.

Agent Lyons was there just a short time before deciding that this young fellow could guide him westward to the Chouteau trading post on the Verdigris River in Oklahoma. A. P. Chouteau was the head of about 2,000 Osage Indians who lived in the vicinity. The Cherokee agent felt that the Osages and Cherokees needed to have an understanding about hunting grounds. This would be the first time Jesse acted as a guide, except for the times he had brought his grandfather and uncle west.

Colonel Auguste Pierre Chouteau was from the St. Louis family, and had been trading all his life. He had moved the Osages westward with him and ruled over them like a king. The two visitors were very impressed with the luxury that they found in this "uncivilized" place. Jesse's grandfather was considered wealthy, but had nothing compared to what was to be found here.

Jesse wandered about while the two men were talking to the Indian leaders. He was learning Osage words as he waited for the talks to end.

Lyons and Chouteau got along fine, having both known Andy Jackson. But Jesse was making a good impression on the trading king too. The man noticed his friendliness and his business sense so much that he asked Jesse to return for other visits. This was wonderful news to Jesse. Perhaps this master trader could help him get started, for he had already decided that he'd make his fortune in trading.

On a recent trip and again in Fort Smith, Jesse heard that Mexico was giving land grants to United States men who wanted to move to Texas. One soldier told him, "A fellow named Stephen F. Austin, from Missouri, got permission to bring 300 settlers in — and to get titles to their land."

"When is he bringing them?"

"Right away."

Jesse remarked, "I met a judge by that name in the city of Little Rock once."

"That's the one."

"He was a likable fellow."

Many other Anglos liked Austin, too, and it wasn't hard for him to get settlers. Much of the old farmland in the South was wearing out, and this caused many leaders to follow Austin. Mexico City issued many titles to land in Texas in the 1820s.

Another Cherokee leader, Chief John Bowles, brought his group from eastern lands to the Angelina, Trinity, and Neches River bottoms to live. Soon they decided to get legal permission to stay. Chief Bowles asked Jesse Chisholm to go with him to Mexico City for deeds. Jesse had never been there before, but was very excited about doing so.

They had no trouble finding the way, but had real trouble getting deeds. They ended up with "squatters' rights," which gave them the right to the land if they lived on it at least five years.

While in Mexico, Jesse had met Santa Anna, who was to become the dictator of Mexico a few years later. This time, Jesse was hearing and learning Spanish words.

Returning home from Mexico City, Jesse found that Sequoyah had come west to get help in having his syllabary recognized. He had been unable to do so in the East. This work had been made into eighty-five characters or syllables which could be taught to bright children in a few days. Jesse, of course, learned to write the Cherokee language quicker than most of the younger kids. He was glad to see his old friend and to know that he had finally succeeded in his life's work.

Some of Sequoyah's syllabary is like the English alphabet, for that was the guide or model he used to record the different sounds. But the sounds are not like the English alphabet because he had no idea what the English alphabet sounded like. He just looked at an old spelling book and some numbers and assigned them to the Cherokee sounds. (A copy of the syllabary can be found next to the glossary.)

Sequoyah had proved to the tribe that his work was usable and that written language could be read by anyone who knew the characters. He did this by having some chiefs tell him a message, which he wrote down while his little daughter was out of the room. When she returned, she read exactly what the men had said. His "talking leaves" really worked. Parents understood this and let him teach the syllabary to their children. Soon Western Cherokee parents had all their children writing in their own language. It was wonderful!

Then when the lame man, Sequoyah, went back east to Tennessee, he was able to teach several leaders the syllabary in just a few lessons. They realized, too, that it was not magic as some had thought, but like the "talking leaves" of the English. It could be read by all who learned it.

The Eastern Cherokees awarded Sequoyah a medal, which he always wore when he "dressed up" after that. They also voted him a small pension so that he would not have to do hard blacksmithing in the future. He became a minor chief and went to Washington to talk about a new treaty. People realized that he was the only person who had single-handedly invented a new alphabet. With this new development, a progressive young man began printing a Cherokee newspaper, called *The Phoenix*.

One day Sequoyah said to the chief of the Eastern Cherokees, "I am lonely for my old friends who live there."

The chief replied, "We'd love to have you here

forever, but I understand how you feel. Good luck. You may see us coming there one day, Things haven't settled down much here."

Sequoyah and his family were welcomed warmly back in the western land. Jesse saw him often after that, and they became real friends.

Since Jesse was now making a good living by trading furs, he decided that he and his mother should move closer to Fort Gibson, an army fort established in Oklahoma Territory in 1825. Indians didn't really like to come to trading posts, so the young fellow found it much easier to take goods to them (for which they paid in furs). Soon he got a peddler's license and a wagon to carry goods in. He was well on his way to making a better living.

It was after this move to Fort Smith that Jesse again ran into Jim Bowie of the Bowie knife fame. Jim and his brother had brought slaves there to sell. Though bringing slaves into the United States was illegal after 1808, trading them was not. These two brothers had traded for them in Louisiana earlier, and now were selling them at the fort. Jesse saw that this loud but likable man was followed by crowds of admirers wherever he went. He decided if he had to be in a fight, it would be good to have Jim Bowie on his side.

Comanches and Apaches often made slaves of captives (whites, blacks, or other Indians). Later on, Jesse would sometimes buy these captives to return them to their families or rightful owners. He didn't always approve of these frontier transactions, but "went along with the crowd." After seeing the bad effects of guns and whiskey on both races, he stopped dealing in both.

7

Sam Houston Returns

By the time Jesse was twenty-one, he was a well-known guide and interpreter who traded with the Creeks, with Chouteau's Osages, with his own Cherokees, and with anyone else in his territory. Even though he was young, he was often called "Old Prairie Jess."

His knowledge of Indian dialects was probably greater than that of any other frontiersman. The demand for his services as guide and interpreter often interfered with his trapping, hunting, and trading. He sometimes resented this, for guides were paid very little — even by the government.

One day Jesse said to his mother, "I am glad you told me once that I could be either white or Indian. But I often have trouble knowing which I am."

Martha Chisholm answered, "You're doing a very good job of being both, Jess."

However, he never got too close to either race. He was a loner, but a very friendly one. Once he did have a short love affair with a Cherokee maiden.

Jesse had begun storing his supplies and furs with Chouteau. He purchased corn to resell and sometimes livestock, or anything else that was in demand. Chouteau had prospered greatly after coming to Oklahoma Territory — as members of his family always did. But he and Jesse lost everything in the Arkansas River flood of 1826. Good-natured Jesse just shrugged it off by saying, "Chouteau still has his credit. I don't."

It didn't take Jesse long to recover his losses. He borrowed a wagon from his uncle and set out with a load of salt, which he sold for quite a profit. Salt was always needed to preserve and season food, and members of his family owned salt springs nearby. Then he thought of providing corn to farmers for half their year's crop. This, too, was successful. Jesse would never deal just in furs from then on. He would branch out into many areas.

Meanwhile, back in the United States, Andy Jackson was elected president in 1828. Although his big victory at Horseshoe Bend had been possible chiefly through the help of Cherokees, he still kept moving them out of their homeland in the East. At one time these Indians occupied large areas of Georgia, South and North Carolina, Kentucky, and Tennessee, and lesser parts of Virginia, West Virginia, and Alabama. Now they were crowded into about one-third of that area.

When the Cherokees took their case to the Supreme Court, Chief Justice John Marshall ruled in favor of the Cherokees. They were very happy, but Jackson didn't intend for them to win. He was heard to say, "John Marshall has made his ruling. Now let him enforce it." And, of course, he could not without the president's help.

Jesse, who had always admired Andy Jackson when he saw him at his grandfather's inn at Knoxville, Tennessee, now could not understand how he could be so hard-hearted to these former friends of his. He began to wonder about Sam Houston's friendship with Andy.

He said to his mother, "Why doesn't Colonneh talk to General Jackson? He must understand how we feel."

"Yes, but have you ever suggested that to Sam?"

"I'm not one to make suggestions to Sam Houston. And perhaps he's not one to make suggestions to Andy Jackson. Colonneh probably wouldn't have been elected to the United States House of Representatives if Jackson hadn't helped him campaign."

"And then the governorship of Tennessee later," his mother added.

One day Jesse got a copy of the new newspaper *The Cherokee Phoenix,* which was being printed in New Echota, Georgia, the capital of the Eastern Cherokees. He was pleased and thrilled to think of the happiness of Sequoyah over the paper — a bilingual one that Cherokees could read. Of course the paper was usually a month old before it reached him, but it was always full of news about people he knew.

Jesse rushed to his mother and read, "Governor Sam Houston, who is running for reelection for governor of Tennessee, announces his engagement to Miss Eliza Allen."

"That is good. Colonneh is doing well. I hope he is very happy. Are you ever going to get married, Jess?"

He laughed. "Who knows?"

But Martha's good wishes were not to come true. In two months the *Phoenix* announced that Sam and Eliza had separated and that he was resigning as governor. All kinds of rumors reached the Western Cherokees at the fort, the main one being that Colonneh would form a huge Indian army to capture Texas land from Mexico. Then word came that Colonneh was coming to join the Cherokees, as he had done once before when he was troubled.

All the Rogers-Chisholm-Jolly clan met the boat when a very drunk Sam Houston staggered off. Chief Jolly took care of his adopted son and helped him overcome this big blow to his pride.

In a few months, Sam had regained his self-respect and was again full of grand plans for his future. He would make a fortune trading, as the Chouteaus had done, and then he would represent the Cherokees and other tribes in Washington, D.C. Before the year was out, Colonneh had quit worrying about Eliza and was looking lovingly at Tiana, Jesse's aunt, whom Sam had known when she was a child back in Tennessee.

Colonneh soon married Tiana in a Cherokee wedding ceremony. At that time the wedding ceremony was simple. The bride brought the groom a green ear of corn, meaning she would be taking the job of raising vegetables for the family. The groom brought her venison and promised to hunt meat for the family. Then they each brought a blanket, which the chief joined together, declaring them man and wife.

After the rite, Jesse said to Sam, "I never expected you to be my uncle, back in Tennessee."

"Well, you never know how things will turn out. You might even get married someday."

Soon Sam started a trading post, after some confusion about whether Sam was a Cherokee or not (in October the tribe had made him a member). This store building was called Wigwam Neosho and it became a popular meeting place for both whites and Indians. Often when Sam was in Washington, Jesse and Tiana kept things running at the business. Jesse himself stayed busy, and early in 1830 was awarded a contract to furnish corn for Fort Gibson. This was big business in those days.

Meanwhile, the Cherokees were not the only group from the Five Civilized Tribes to be having a hard time keeping their land. About 800 Creeks from the southeastern United States were herded into the area near Fort Gibson. These people were not like the Cherokees already there; they were pitifully poor, sick, and hungry. Jesse watched them and made a pledge to himself to help Indians whenever he could. He vowed to do everything short of rebelling against the government.

While Sam was again in Washington, Colonel Matthew Arbuckle, that rather strange commander of the soldiers at Fort Gibson, got excited about tales of the discovery of gold in the Wichita Mountains. Knowing that Jesse was a good guide, he came to him one day and said, "Young man, could you guide me and a group to the Wichita Mountains?"

"Yes, I could, but why are you going?"

"To find that gold I keep hearing about."

"Colonel, you won't find any."

"But we might."

After some delay, Jesse agreed to go on the "wild goose chase" for several months. Just as Jesse feared, there was no gold, and they had wasted several months. Perhaps Jesse knew that Indians had always been telling whites that there was gold farther on, to get them off of their land.

As soon as he returned from this trip, Jesse agreed to help Robert Bean lay out a road to the new Fort Towson post, which the government had decided was very important. Towson was being established about 150 miles southwest of Fort Smith, almost on the Red River and the beginning of Mexican land.

Sam Houston and Jesse both wanted peace between Indians and the United States. Each tried in his own way to iron out the problems. Jesse probably succeeded better than Houston in Oklahoma Territory.

Sam had gone to Congress dressed as a Cherokee; that is why we often see pictures of him dressed in the tunic and turban of that day's Cherokees. Many congressmen and the secretary of the army resented this dress and caused trouble for old Sam. However, Andy Jackson was always able to get him out of his fusses.

At about this time, many frontiersmen decided it would be good to "Go to Texas," and hundreds of Southern farmers, with worn-out land, agreed with them. Sam Houston, whose dreams for his business in Oklahoma were not working out so well, caught the Texas Fever, and talked it over with Tiana. She didn't want to go. They decided to "split the blanket," or get an Indian divorce. Sam left all his property to Tiana, and departed on friendly terms.

Going by to see Jesse on his way south, Sam said, "I can't see why you don't go with me, Jess. Texas is the land of the future."

"That may be true, Colonneh, but I've got a good business here, and don't want to start over."

"Have you been to see James Edwards at his store?"

"Yes, and he's very friendly. Maybe I can get to be a partner. Besides that, he has a pretty daughter."

Sam laughed. "I understand. What's her name?"

"You are not going to like it. It's Eliza."

"No, that's not my favorite name. But we won't hold that against her," he said. Sam never explained to anyone why his marriage to Eliza Allen didn't work out.

Meanwhile, Jesse's Cherokee friends were upset with him for not taking their side in a boundary dispute with the nearby Creeks. He, as usual, didn't let it bother him too much, for he knew they would forgive him soon — when they needed him.

8

Jesse Works for Peace

Jesse Chisholm's creaky peddler's cart often made its peaceful way across Indian Territory and into Texas. During his lifetime, he was adopted by twelve different tribes, and eventually spoke fourteen Indian dialects (as well as good English, and some Spanish and French). His interpreting services were constantly in demand. When he was on a mission, Jesse rode a black and white spotted mare, and wore fringed buckskins. Only his red hair revealed him as being part white.

Sometimes Jesse paid to get runaway slaves or kidnapped children back from the Indians and return them to their rightful owners or families. Slavery had existed from our country's beginning until after the Civil War. Though Jesse was sometimes considered to be a slaver, he knew how badly the owners or families wanted the people back, and how badly the Indians needed a little bit of money. Many of the Indians owned slaves, though this wasn't widely known.

In 1833, another flood on the Arkansas River brought more losses to Jesse and all those in the area. This hardship, along with the constant bickering of nearby tribes, made Jesse want to "get away from it all" for a while. All his life he'd found traveling fun, and being in his late twenties didn't change that. Just as he was about to leave, Sam Houston asked for his help. Now a Texas leader but also still acting as agent of the Indians, Sam persuaded Jesse to round up a bothersome tribe of Comanches for a treaty in San Antonio. Then Sam didn't show up, leaving Jesse to apologize to the "terrors of the Plains." Luckily, he was able to keep them peaceful with a promise of future meetings.

As soon as he got back to his work, Sam sent Jesse another message to "round up all the wild Indians" for an important meeting with government officials, soldiers, and guests. President Jackson and Congress had decided to make a big display of power by creating a new cavalry unit to show the Indians. They would be called the "United States Dragoons." Their uniforms were outlandish: dark blue jackets, gray pants with yellow stripes, orange sashes, and tall black hats with yellow stripes and drooping white feathers.

Old Colonel Arbuckle said to Jesse, "Did you

ever see anything so awful looking? The Congress must be out of its mind!"

"Yes, and if I understand the orders right, they'll have to stay here until they are ready for battle or whatever."

"There is no room for them here. They'll have to be put up in tents," the colonel answered.

"And winter will be here soon. They're going to have a hard time."

Jesse had no idea how hard a time they would have. There were 500 of them when they all arrived — brand new troops with no knowledge of life in the army or of Indians. Many of them had "joined up" just for fun and were ready to quit when they found out how hard the job was going to be. It took six months to get them ready for the expedition. Their commander, Colonel Henry Dodge, was soon replaced by General Henry Leavenworth, and the expedition was named for the two men. They were to make a strong show of strength to all the Plains Indians.

By July, they had crossed into Texas. Insects were very bothersome, the heat was terrible, and the men (including General Leavenworth) began coming down with some mysterious disease. Jesse and Colonel Dodge knew that it would be bad if the Indians learned that they were experiencing illness and death. They set up a camp for the sick and left a group of men to look after them until the army's return.

On sighting a big Comanche camp at their

first meeting, Jesse said to the colonel, "They are friendly. We'll have no trouble here if we're careful."

"How do you know that?"

"I know this old chief. Had they intended to fight, they would have attacked long before now."

When the old chief saw Jesse, he seated him beside himself on the side of the Comanches, so that the colonel wouldn't have him to help interpret. Though this surprised and upset the colonel, he need not have worried, for Jesse reworded all the conversation so that it came out friendlier from each side. Thanks to Jesse, the old colonel's usual manner of giving orders became softer, and the old chief's slow decisions were reworded to suit the army. Jesse, already of great value to the Indians, was now being seen as an asset to the United States Army — not just for his knowledge of languages, but also for his peacemaking ability.

The Comanches agreed to guide them to the Wichitas, some seventy miles away. This tribe, also called the Pawnee Picts, were not "wild Indians" but peaceful settlers with good houses and farms. They welcomed the soldiers and fed them well for several days until other tribes came and the peace talks started.

Kiowas came in as the session began, but when they found out that the army had brought some Osages along, they were ready to fight. So were the Osages.

Jesse whispered to Colonel Dodge, "Now is the time to bring out the little Kiowa girl you had me buy from the Osages before we started."

"I was about to forget that. Maybe that'll settle the Kiowas down," the colonel said.

The Kiowas were so thrilled to see their kidnapped child, and to get her back without having to pay, that they laughed, cried, and forgot their anger. Dodge and Jesse smiled at each other and went on with the meeting.

Before they left the Comanche camp, Jesse had paid the Comanches for two children, one white and one black, that he had seen there. Now he presented them to Colonel Dodge and everybody was again delighted.

It seemed that they might make a good treaty after all. But Colonel Dodge was not empowered to sign the treaty; all they did was to get the various tribes to promise to send representatives to the fort later. It seemed to Jesse that this was a backward way of doing things, but he could never make sense of all that the United States Army did. Then he found out that Colonel Dodge was getting ill, too, and hurried back to the fort. Jesse had gained a good reputation as a peacemaker and trailblazer — and one who held the promise of future treaties.

The artist George Catlin painted hundreds of portraits of this expedition, but not one of Jesse, who "never found time" to pose for him.

This meeting of the Dragoons and Indians in

1834, and the ensuing treaty at Fort Gibson, did not end Jesse's interpreting and peacemaking activities. For the next thirty-three years, he was always in demand by both Indians and the United States government.

Because of his honest trading with them, and his appreciation of their love of beads, trinkets, brightly colored materials, and rituals, many tribes sought Jesse out. However, Jesse's living came chiefly from the sale of hides he traded and sold. He was the only person who knew not to schedule treaty meetings that would interfere with the time that the Plains Indians followed the buffalo on their migrations. He was one of the few whites about whom they said, "He had a straight tongue," meaning he was honest with them.

In the 1800s, much of our country was still "wild," and huge herds of buffalo roamed the plains. Coming back to Fort Griffin, Jesse and the Dodge party had to spend one entire day waiting for an almost endless group of buffalo to pass by. Catlin, the artist, was so delighted that he began sketching immediately. This and the herd itself kept the tired party amused for hours. Imagine 10,000 animals lumbering along, and an artist trying to paint them!

Of course, the buffalo were the real reason for so much of the trouble between the Indians and whites. Most Plains Indians depended almost entirely on the buffalo. The buffalo provided meat for food, leather for clothing, hides to make tepees for shelter, and buffalo chips for fuel to cook meals.

Whites, in general, did not appreciate the importance of the buffalo to the Indians, and saw nothing wrong with just killing them for sport and leaving the meat to rot. Later, when railroads were being built across the nation, thousands of these majestic animals were shot just to get them out of the way (and later for their hides and bones). It is no surprise that the Indians were so enraged by all this carnage that they fought against it. This brought about many treaties — treaties that were easily and often broken.

9

War in Texas!

When Sam Houston left Jesse for Texas in 1832, he knew that conditions were very unsettled in that Mexican land. Mexico had only been free from Spain since 1821, and had not learned to govern herself, nor Texas, yet. Thousands of Anglos had rushed into the land when it was opened to settlement. There was much confusion in land grants, and many of the newcomers had no legal right to take the land. Of course, Texas Indian tribes still claimed that all their hunting grounds were being invaded. They were ready for war with the newcomers and with each other.

But Sam Houston was never one to run away from an argument or a fight, and he knew what he was getting into. When he saw Jesse in San Antonio, he told him how Stephen F. Austin, who had become the Texas leader, had tried to settle problems and keep peace. However, it was hard to keep peace when Mexico's leaders kept changing and new men kept making new laws. Two things in the new laws really bothered the Texans: that slavery was illegal and that more Mexican ex-soldiers, ex-convicts, and very poor people would be sent into the territory.

Sam said, "You know how you'd feel if convicts were moved into your area."

Jesse responded, "Not too well."

Sam reminded Jesse that he himself had given his only slave to Tiana when they divorced. Jesse, of course, had bought slave hostages from Indians to return to their owners many times. Most well-to-do settlers had brought their slaves with them. Sam said that Austin had been able to get the law changed somewhat: they could keep the ones they had, but couldn't import more. He added, "Austin is a very good man."

Jesse answered, "So it seems. I was well impressed the only time I saw him."

Jesse had returned to his Oklahoma trading routes, but continued to hear of the Texas troubles. It seemed that after one inspection trip by authorities, the Mexican government was sending more and more soldiers to every fort in Texas. In order to discuss solutions, Texans held a convention to decide what to do. They decided to send Austin to Mexico City to talk with the authorities.

The next year, when Sam stopped at Fort Gibson on his way to meet with Andy Jackson about Texas problems, he said to Jesse, "We decided to ask Mexico to make Texas a separate state from Coahuila."

"Coahuila is the part of Mexico just below the Rio Grande, isn't it?"

"Yes," responded Sam. "I helped to write a constitution for us."

"Isn't that going to cause trouble?"

"When we sent Austin down, we felt sure he could keep peace," explained Sam. "But the Mexicans had made Santa Anna president, and he was a horse of a different color."

"He's that fellow I met who thinks he's Napoleon. . ."

"The very one!" exclaimed Sam. "Now he's arrested Austin, and we don't know when he'll be back. Texas is being divided into two parties: the War and Peace parties."

"That's too bad," said Jesse. "I'm still trying to keep the tribes quiet."

"That's what you should do. We surely don't need Indian wars too."

"What's Austin been charged with?" asked Jesse.

"Nothing yet. I'm going to talk to Andy about all this."

Jesse really couldn't understand how Houston was still so fond of Jackson, after all the things he was doing to the Cherokees and other tribes. But he wasn't asked for his opinion, and surely wouldn't give it until he was.

"Do you remember Jim Bowie?" asked Sam.

"The man with the good knife?"

"Yes. He's been in Texas some years now. He's not just a good fighter, but a very successful man — land owner, slave dealer, friend of the rich, and the son-in-law of the aristocratic and wealthy Mexican mayor of San Antonio."

Later, Jesse heard that Austin was kept in prison over a year, and came back to find that Houston had been made the commander of the rag-tag Texas Army. Now it seemed that all Texans belonged to the War Party — even Stephen F. Austin.

Both Mexicans and Texans tried to get various Indian tribes to help out in the oncoming war. Jesse advised all the neighboring groups to stay out of Texas and not to get involved in a "white man's war."

Jesse himself was getting involved — romantically, that is, with Eliza Edwards. Her father was Scottish and mother was Creek. Jesse and Eliza were married the same year that the big battles were fought for Texas independence, 1836. It was a strange union, though, for Jesse was away from home almost all the time. They lived at and looked after the Edwards Store for two years.

While beginning trade at the Texas Brazos River post, Jesse heard the rest of the story about the Texas Revolution. There had been several skirmishes over cannons, land grants, ports, and government before the Battle of San Antonio in late 1835. Mexican General Cos, knowing he could not win against such an energetic group of Texans, surrendered the city and returned to Mexico. But the Texans' joy of victory was not to last long. It was rumored that General Santa Anna himself was actually coming into their land with a huge, well-equipped army.

The Texas Army was anything but a real army. The men were volunteers who came and went almost at will. They were scattered — some had just returned from an unsuccessful expedition to the Rio Grande area; some were in San Antonio; and Sam Houston himself was in Gonzales. There was very little discipline and no line of command. It looked very bad for the Texans.

In spite of heavy winter rains, Santa Anna came steadily on, arriving in San Antonio much earlier than expected. Sam Houston, knowing how few men were in the city, sent Jim Bowie with a message for the soldiers there to blow up the old Alamo mission. It would have been a stronghold if the Mexicans had it. He also ordered them all to come eastward. But Jim Bowie and Colonel William B. Travis decided not to obey. They felt that more of their army could get to them before Santa Anna got there. A few Texans did arrive, but not nearly enough — and then Santa Anna came much faster than they thought he could.

On February 3, 1836, the huge, grand-looking Mexican army arrived. Sharing the command of the Alamo, Travis and Bowie (now very ill) and their brave group fought very valiantly for thirteen days. They had expected Colonel James Fannin to come to their aid with his 400 men from the old fort near Goliad, but he did not.

On the morning of March 6, the Mexicans finally scaled the wall. At Santa Anna's orders, they killed all 183 men left inside. Santa Anna allowed a woman and some children to escape — to tell Texans what had happened. It was a great victory for the Mexicans, but one which gave the Texans the powerful battle cry: "Remember the Alamo!"

Sam Houston really worried about the defeat at the Alamo. It looked hopeless for the Texans. He quickly sent word to Fannin in South Texas to leave the fort and join the rest of the army. But Fannin was too slow. He fought a losing battle with a huge section of the Mexican army, and surrendered, expecting to have the men treated as prisoners of war. On the next Sunday (one week before Easter), all the men (more than 300) were marched out of Goliad and shot. This added another phrase to the battle cry: "Remember the Alamo! Remember Goliad!"

Jesse was sorry to hear about these two tragedies. Before long, his messengers told him that Houston was running from Santa Anna's army. It was called a Runaway Scrape. "All the people who've settled in Central Texas have left their homes and are tagging along with Houston's pitiful army and are fleeing to Louisiana or somewhere!" the messengers reported.

"That can't be right," Jesse said. "Sam would not run from a fight. He must have some plan he's following."

And Jesse was right. In the next news, he learned that after calming the scared population, Houston had turned to face "the little Napoleon of the West" at San Jacinto. In eighteen minutes the Texans had defeated Santa Anna in one of the most important battles in United States history.

Jesse smiled and said, "I knew he could do it. They'll probably elect him president of the new Republic of Texas next."

And that is just what happened in October of that same year.

10

Many Trails of Tears

While all this activity was going on in Texas, Jesse's home was still with the Creeks at the Edwards Store. His marriage was going well and business was flourishing.

Jesse and Sequoyah were still trying to keep peace among the many tribes. The old man thought that Indians should do as the whites did: sign the treaties and work out the details later. He and Jesse often discussed the boundaries with many tribal groups. Ocassionally Sequoyah was sent to Washington to help negotiate treaties, and he was president of the convention that made peace among the three groups of Cherokees. But Jesse was always the one to work with the different tribes because of his understanding of their languages.

In 1837 the master trader Chouteau asked

Jesse to help with the Comanches, Kiowas, and Apaches (and probably with the Osages, since he was their leader). Jesse had hardly finished this when Sam Houston called him to the new Texas capital in Houston.

Jesse said, "Why can't they let me get back to work? I have to make a living."

Sequoyah said, "Perhaps this has something to do with Chief Bowles that you told me about."

"Perhaps. But he just might want to talk."

Houston, as president of the new republic, continued to stay on friendly terms with Indians, particularly with the Cherokees. And this did, indeed, have to do with Chief Bowles.

That same year, Jesse and Eliza had their first child, a healthy boy that they named William. Jesse was sorry he couldn't spend more time with his family. He loved children, especially his daughter who was born later, and the thirteen others whom they adopted.

Jesse had found these orphaned children, some Cherokees, some from other tribes, and he'd bring them home, saying to Eliza, "I just can't stand to think of their being hungry and cold." She would always reply that he'd done the right thing. He was constantly helping people who had problems.

Back in the East, young John Ross, a wealthy, part Cherokee man, had been elected principal chief in 1828. The capital of the Eastern Cherokees was then in New Echota, Georgia, but the tribes were scattered over several states. Ross was such a good chief that he kept the job until his death in 1866.

The good chief made many trips to Washington, D. C., defending the Cherokees' rights to their eastern lands. He wasn't successful, however, and in the same year that Jesse heard of the Texans winning their independence, he heard of the Cherokees losing their land in the East. All of the Five Civilized Tribes had this fate. The Choctaws moved westward in 1821, the Creeks in 1836, then the Chickasaws and Seminoles the next year (that is, those Seminoles who didn't hide in the Florida swamps).

For years John Ross had tried to get Jackson to change his mind, and to pay a bigger price for the land. The Cherokees really expected him to be able to do this, but in the end, he couldn't. Jackson told the Indians that he'd have the army move them all, after a small group of men led by Boudinot signed a treaty that most of the Cherokees disapproved of. This group left early for the West and were soon followed by 2,000 others. However, most of the Cherokees waited to be put out by the army.

When the United States Army arrived, all the remaining Cherokees were snatched from their farms and imprisoned in forts, with very few belongings. They were so crowded together and the food was so bad that many became very ill.

When John Ross returned from Washington,

he was able to get some of the bad conditions changed. He was also able to help make plans for evacuation, and to delay the departure until fall, so that they could avoid the extreme heat.

Many of these people talked to Jesse when they finally arrived in Oklahoma, almost six months after beginning the trip. John Burnett, a young soldier who went with them, wrote a complete account of this cruel trip. (The letter, written for his descendants much later, is now in the Museum of Cherokee History in Cherokee, North Carolina.)

Not quite all the Cherokees went on this horrible trip. About 500 were allowed to stay. And about the same number escaped from the stockades and fled to the mountains. But there were almost 17,000 who went. Hundreds had to walk most of the almost 900 miles to Oklahoma Indian Territory. The journey began in October 1838, from the Smoky Mountains. By November they ran into sleet. John Burnett wrote:

"The trail of the exiles was a trail of death. They had to sleep in the wagons or on the ground without a fire. And I have known as many as 22 of them to die in one night of pneumonia due to ill treatment, cold, and exposure. Among this number was the beautiful Christian wife of John Ross."

There were about 4,000 deaths, and the bodies had to be buried beside the road. It was a horrible experience, one that became known as "The Trail of Tears" and "The Place Where We Cried."

The arrival of this group in Oklahoma created more work for Jesse. He said to his wife, "There are now three groups of our people. First we had us, the Old Timers, then came Boudinot and his group, now all of John Ross' bunch."

"You'll be able to help, Jesse. You'll see," Eliza assured him.

Because John Ross' group was the largest, at election time he was elected principal chief of all. Their laws had changed since the first group left; so there was a good bit of confusion. Neither Jesse, nor Sequoyah, nor John Ross knew the answers to all their problems. But before agreements could be signed, unknown assassins killed the three leaders of Boudinot's group. Jesse grieved about this, and then about the death of his friend and master trader Chouteau. Now the Osages were leaderless too. This would be another problem.

While Jesse was worrying about the Cherokee problems, the yen to travel hit him again. He came in from a trading trip very tired one day.

He said to his wife, "I've always wanted to go to California. This would be a good time to do so. I can now see about getting trade opened with those people out there."

"That would be exciting, but how would you get there? You've said that desert travel is horrible."

"I wouldn't have to go overland all the way. It would be easier to get through Mexico to the Pacific and then by boat up the coast."

And so, he and another trader went south, having fun just sightseeing at first. They went through San Antonio to see the Alamo and hear more about the tragedy there. Jesse's ability to speak Spanish made the trip easier, but there were many new Indian dialects. The land was quite different sometimes.

"They have so much cacti in this country," he said, and then realized that the desert extended on down into Mexico.

Later his friend said, "I never saw so many trees with thorns all over them. And so few people."

Jesse answered, "But there are some of the prettiest flowers I ever saw. And these mountains are a lot higher than those in Oklahoma and Tennessee."

When they finally reached the Pacific Coast, they went by boat from Mazatlan, Mexico, to San Francisco. Then they saw many trading houses along the California coast where the mission priests had settled. From San Diego, they started homeward, crossing much more desert land. They found no pretty waterfalls here, as they had in western Mexico. It was a long trip.

When Jesse arrived home he told his children, "I never saw so much beautiful scenery, so many pretty waterfalls, and such a big canyon (Copper Canyon) in my life. But I don't know whether or not I want to start a trading route to California." And he never did.

Before the California trip, Jesse met Sequoyah one day. The old man was getting sick and weak, but was still mentally active.

He said, "Jesse, this place is getting so crowded, I don't like it anymore. They've been telling me that farther down in Mexico there is good free land to be had by anyone. Why don't you go with me to see about it? I've always wondered about the stories that I hear of Cherokee migration there long ago."

"Sequoyah, I don't see how I can go now."

"Perhaps I can get others to go, if you can draw me a map."

Jesse drew a map as best he could. He really didn't think the old one would go. But he heard soon that a few men, including one of Sequoyah's sons, had decided to go with him. They set out at once.

It was two years later that Chief Ross was still so worried about Sequoyah's continued absence that he talked Jesse into going to Mexico to look for him. There Jesse found that the old leader became tired and sick near a cave. His son Tessy and all the others except one man, Standing Rock, went into town. They thought he was safe. But the weather, sickness, and age caught up with him. This wonderful old man, who had done so much for the Cherokees, inventing their alphabet, attending many peace treaty meetings, and presiding at the convention which united the three western groups, died alone in a strange land away from the people whom he had helped all his life.

Jesse learned all this from Standing Rock and the other survivors. His report, dated April 12, 1845, said Sequoyah had died in August 1843, with one friend with him; he was buried. His son was on the Brazos River and would return in the fall. Three Indians signed the report, along with Jesse and another witness.

Chief Ross had also persuaded the Cherokee agent P. M. Butler to send a search party to look for Sequoyah. Its report in May said about the same thing, but added that Standing Rock had witnessed the burial.

When Oklahoma came into the Union in 1907, they chose his statue to put in the congressional Statuary Hall of Fame in the United States Capitol. They remembered how great Sequoyah was, and people in Oklahoma still do.

11

Jesse's Final Peacemaking

Jesse continued his peacemaking and interpreting all through the 1840s, often at Sam Houston's suggestion. The most feared tribes were the Comanches, who moved about on the plains. In Texas, Chief Bowles was following Houston's instructions in keeping the Cherokees and other groups quiet. But when a larger area became involved, Sam asked Jesse to round up the interested parties. In 1843 he was able to get nine tribes to meet at Tehuacana Creek in McLennan County. However, little came of this meeting.

As long as Sam Houston was president of the republic, the Indians were fairly peaceful, knowing that they had a friend in him. But in Texas, a president could not succeed himself, and Mirabeau B. Lamar was elected next. Everybody knew Lamar was not friendly to the Indians.

Jesse said, "He's just like Andy Jackson. He thinks all Indians are bad."

Almost immediately, war broke out between the Indians and whites. No tribe fared worse than poor Chief Bowles' Cherokees. More than twenty years before, he had gone to Mexico trying to get a legal land grant but had failed, only getting "squatters' rights." Then he had signed a treaty with Houston, which the Senate would not approve, even though Houston had personally signed the document and sealed the bargain with a sword and sash to the chief.

Lamar decided to force all Indians to leave Texas and go to Indian Territory in Oklahoma. When they reached the Neches River, the Cherokees, knowing that they were being treated unfairly, turned and fought. Of course, they lost, and Chief Bowles was killed, wearing the sash and sword that Colonneh had given him. Sorrowfully, Jesse heard of this event.

Jesse's next attempt at peace was to bring thirty-two tribes together for a treaty in Council Grove, Oklahoma, a place where he would open a trading post later. This treaty was a bit more successful. But the one he enjoyed the most was on the Concho River in 1850. At that get-together all the tribes dug a huge hole in the ground and the chiefs threw into it their tomahawks, scalpers, and fresh corn—as a promise of future peace and agriculture.

While all this tribal work and his usual trading were going on, Jesse was having personal problems. His wife, Eliza, died of smallpox, leaving Jesse to look after their sixteen children. Although he'd always been on friendly terms with both Indians and whites, he'd kept his family apart from both. Now he was very lonely.

He soon hired a neighboring widow to be a substitute mother and housekeeper for the children while he returned to his trading. This arrangement worked well for about a year, until he married Sari McQueen, a part-Creek woman whom he'd known for a long time. Neighbors said that the marriage was too quick and wouldn't last. Twenty-one years later, when Jesse died, he was still married to this good woman.

One of his children asked him one day, "Daddy, how many homes have you had?"

"Well, I lived in the Smoky Mountains before we moved to Arkansas. After my father disappeared, your grandmother Martha and I moved to the Fort Gibson area of Oklahoma. After Eliza and I were married, we lived at Edwards Store on Little River. When Sari and I got married, we moved to Asher, where I already had a trading post. I like living near Indians."

But it seemed that Indians were always between two sides in some white man's war, with each side trying to get the tribal help. Jesse remained a peacemaker, not a warrior.

He stayed neutral when Southern states began getting out of the Union, and when several tribes came to him for help in deciding what to do. He kept saying, "Don't get into a white man's war." He knew that whichever side the Indians helped, they'd fight hard, lose many lives, and then be treated badly when it was all over.

Sam Houston, their Colonneh, was having his troubles too. He was a United States senator when the Civil War started brewing. Because one of the causes of the war was slavery, and its extension into new territory, and because Houston had voted against its extension into Kansas, many Texans were now against Houston. When he got back into Texas and ran for state governor, he was defeated in 1859. But two years later, people forgot about that and voted for "good old Sam" again. Now he, like Jesse, wanted to stay neutral in the big struggle.

Most Cherokees remained neutral, but Stand Watie, one of their leaders, was persuaded by the South, or Confederacy, to join its side. A good-sized group of young tribesmen went with him. John Ross stayed out of the quarrel for a while, too, but eventually went with the Confederacy.

By late 1861, at the urging of Creeks, Shawnees, and other Cherokees, Jesse led a group out of the territory and into Kansas, where there was less danger of being caught in the struggle.

He heard that Sam Houston had been put out of the governorship when he refused to agree to the state's secession from the Union.

Jesse said to his wife, "Colonneh is just like me. He just can't decide what to do."

But Jesse did decide soon, taking the families and his own in wagons to the Wichita area of Kansas. It was true that they didn't get into the fighting, but the group had so little money that he spent most of his time trying to care for them. For two years, he neglected his trading business. By 1863, he was so tired and weak that he developed pneumonia. In those days, pneumonia was considered fatal. Stephen F. Austin had died of it earlier.

During the six months that Jesse was ill, he got news that Colonneh had retired to Huntsville, Texas, and had died, a disillusioned old man.

When Jesse's health improved a little, he began making trips back for supplies for the poor followers. His reputation as an honest peacemaker was so well-known that he often crossed battlefields. Sentries from both sides let him pass freely, saying only, "It's just Old Prairie Jess. Let him through."

When Jesse did get back to his trading, he heard that some of the Confederate forts were buying cattle and horses. He rounded up all his animals and started to Shreveport, Louisiana.

Arriving in Shreveport, he went to the man in charge of supplies and said, "I'm Jesse Chisholm, a friend of Sam Houston. I hear that some of your men knew Houston."

"The man you want is named Durant. He's always talking about Houston."

Jesse knew Durant, too, but had not heard that he was in charge of supplying materials for the fort. He was happy to find that the pay for his cattle and horses was more than he'd expected. But the pay was in Confederate money, which had to be spent in Louisiana. Buying everything that he'd be able to trade, Jesse rushed back and was in business again.

Back at the trading post, he told a friend, "That trip was fine. I'll get more animals and try it again."

However, his second trip wasn't so successful. He couldn't find anything to buy or trade, for the South was running out of everything and was really losing the war. He went back to Kansas with a chest full of worthless Confederate money. He laughed and said, "I never had so much money, but nothing to buy."

When the war was over in 1865, it became Jesse Chisholm's sad duty to find Stand Watie, the Cherokee leader of the Confederate group, and tell him that the South had lost. Stand was still fighting two months after Lee had surrendered. Jesse found him at Fort Towson and broke the news.

Watie said, "I can't believe it."

"Well, it's true. The surrender was signed two weeks ago."

"And we lost?"

"Yes."

Then both men cried, Watie wondering what would happen to Indians and himself, and Jesse knowing what would happen to all of them. Soon they both took their followers and went back home to Oklahoma.

The years after the Civil War were very hard for Southerners. There was no money, no government, and no hope for the future. But one thing they did have in Texas was wild cattle.

From Spanish mission days these animals had been turned loose and had multiplied on lush grassland. There were millions to be had for the taking. Smart cowmen saw the possibilities here, but there were no markets in the South. They learned that northern packing plants would buy all the cattle that drovers could get to them. In driving cattle to market, the cowboys took the easiest trails possible and developed trails to be followed by the next herds. Three of the best known trails were the Goodnight-Loving, Western, and Chisholm.

The fact that Jesse Chisholm was not a cattleman but a trader is amusing. He traded anything there was a market for, to anyone who would buy. One of his trading routes became the Chisholm Trail, so named by Texas cowboys who extended it farther than he had made it. The part that he actually made was from his home in Council Grove, Oklahoma, to the Wichita area in Kansas (where he had lived during the Civil War). The only time Jesse escorted a huge herd of cattle along the trail was when he overtook someone else's herd. He went along with them from the Red River in Texas to his trading post in Oklahoma.

Jesse had laid out his trail in 1865, but by 1867 the entire passage from the Rio Grande Valley in Texas to Abilene, Kansas, was in use. The Chisholm Trail eventually passed through San Antonio, Austin, Waco, Fort Worth to the Red River, then through Indian Territory and entered Kansas at Caldwell and went on to Abilene (a branch went to Ellsworth).

One reason that the millions of Texas Longhorns traveled the trail was that a smart businessman named McCoy was able to get the railroad to stop in Abilene for his cattle. This stop resulted in a shorter route for the sale of cattle. He may also be responsible for the trail's being named for Chisholm too. Oddly enough, the thousands of cowboys who came over the Chisholm Trail had never heard of Jesse Chisholm.

When Jesse returned home after the Civil War, he found that John Ross had died in Washington, D. C. while still trying to work on peace for the Cherokees.

Jesse said, "We've lost a great one. I think he was the smartest man I ever knew."

"Even smarter than Sequoyah?" his wife asked.

"Yes. Sequoyah really had a one-track brain. John Ross was well-rounded."

Jesse himself was contacted again by the United States government and asked to bring the Kiowas and Comanches together. The two tribes were more hostile than they had been in years. The reasons for this extra hostility had to do with the coming of the railroads and the killing of the buffalo. The wild Plains Indians could not survive without the buffalo. Jesse understood this more than most people. He was finally persuaded to take on this last treaty. After all, his many Indian dialects made him the ablest man to work out an understanding.

The Indians and the army met at Medicine Lodge, Kansas, with both sides putting on a big show of force. The soldiers wore splendid blue uniforms. They had drilled for the impression, and their guns were shining in the sun. The half-naked Indians put on a show of wonderful horsemanship. Each side was impressed by the other, and both really appreciated the work that Jesse Chisholm did. He kept thinking of the many times he had this same job, having worked hard only to have the treaties broken quickly.

Jesse was now in his sixties. He was tired mentally and physically from the Medicine Lodge meeting. Always a joyful hunter, Jesse joined a group of friends for a hunt on the Canadian River in northwestern Oklahoma. They killed a bear and some deer and made a stew. Shortly after eating, Jesse developed food poisoning and died on March 4, 1868.

Many hundreds of whites and Indians mourned his death. They now realized what a great man he had been: a trailblazer and guide, a learner and interpreter of languages, a friend of famous leaders, a merchant, a peacemaker, and a naturalist. He was a truly great man caught between two races.

One of the best compliments paid him was by the modern schoolchildren of Oklahoma, who said on their memorial to Jesse that no one ever left his home hungry or cold.

— Courtesy the artist, Russell Cushman

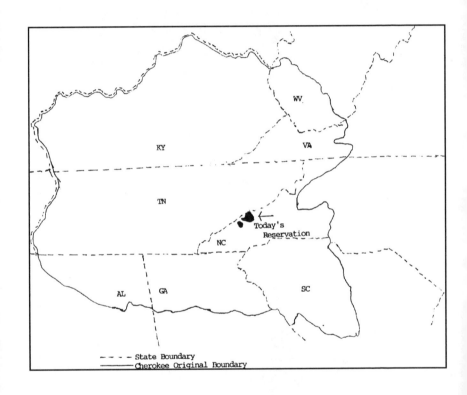

WV

KY

VA

TN

Today's
Reservation

NC

AL

GA

SC

- - - - State Boundary
———— Cherokee Original Boundary

More About the
Eastern Cherokees

Thousands of years ago, wandering primitive tribes of people crossed the land bridge which then existed between Asia and North America into what is now Alaska. They scattered out, eventually going into most parts of North, Central, and South America. One group moved east across Canada and gradually moved southward—taking hundreds of years to do so. We think some of their descendants became Iroquois and others Cherokee (who seemed closely related).

The Cherokees prospered and spread out over parts of the present states of Virginia, West Virginia, Kentucky, Tennessee, North Carolina, South Carolina, Alabama, and Georgia. They may have covered over 135,000 square miles of land at one time. They hunted over most of the area, but also learned to grow crops, making it possible for them to live in stationary homes. Their chief crops were corn, beans, pumpkins, squashes, sunflowers, and gourds. They also grew and used tobacco, though mostly for special rituals. They hunted animals, including deer, bison, bear, turkey, groundhog, rabbit, squirrel, birds, and elk. They also fished and caught frogs from the numerous streams near their settlements.

Before the coming of the white men to this country, Cherokees were already living in cabin-like homes, made of small logs, twigs, vines, and mud, but they quickly adopted the log cabin of the whites. They never lived in tepees as did Plains Indians.

At first their clothes were made of skins and feathers, but then they adopted the tunic (long blouse) and turbans (wrapped cloth head-covering) worn by some whites. They continued to wear deerskin moccasins.

Eventually seven clans were formed: bird, deer, wolf, paint, long hair, blue, and potato. Each of the clans chose a person to represent them on a council, for Cherokees began organizing early. The principal chief was then elected from one clan. Today he serves a four-year term and the councilmen, or women, serve two years. All the members of a clan were considered brothers, and had to marry outside their clan.

Women were very important to the tribe. They or their brothers, rather than a boy's father, were responsible for the son's education.

Women were never considered slaves, as they often were in other more primitive groups. They were the farmers, clothes makers, homemakers, and sometimes chiefs. Men hunted for animals, and fought when necessary. They were responsible for most of the organized government.

Cherokees were the first eastern group to develop a constitutional government, and the only group to develop an alphabet. After Sequoyah developed his Cherokee alphabet, or syllabary, in 1821, most of the children learned quickly to read and write in their native tongue. Shortly after this, a Cherokee newspaper called *The Cherokee Phoenix* was begun in New Echota, Georgia (considered the capital at that time). This paper was published until the tribe was sent westward. Today's official newspaper is *The Cherokee One Feather.* It is published in Cherokee, North Carolina, and carries all the tribal news as well as ordinary local activities, ads, obituaries, letters to the editor, and schedules of local celebrations and powwows. It is an interesting paper which gives an excellent picture of today's Eastern band.

By the 1700s, English colonists had begun spreading their settlements beyond the eastern coasts and were encroaching on lands claimed by the Indians. The first of these to come into Cherokee territory were traders who established posts among friendly tribes. Many of these traders were Scots or Scot-Irish. They usually came alone and soon married Indian women and merged into the tribes. Many of the important Cherokee leaders were only half, quarter, or even eighth Cherokee (John Ross, Sequoyah, and Jesse Chisholm among them).

But the early friendly traders were not the only white men who had contact with the Cherokees and other eastern Indians. As the movement for more land began, frontiersmen began wanting and actually taking Indian lands. Dozens of treaties were made in the late 1700s, only to be broken almost immediately. Peace was disappearing, and many tribes were at constant warfare with the frontiersmen. Even the peaceful Cherokees were sometimes forced into this state of affairs. By the late 1700s, many thoughtful tribesmen were moving westward to new hunting grounds. By the time Andrew Jackson became president of the United States, most of the rest knew they would lose all the eastern land.

John Ross became their leader and spokesman, and in 1828 he was elected the principal chief. For years he tried to negotiate with the federal government, but in the end his efforts were doomed. The removal treaty was signed by a renegade group, who moved westward immediately. John Ross led his 17,000 Cherokees to the west in 1838-39. Four thousand of them died, including Ross' wife, on that horrible, 900-mile exodus in the frigid winter. This trip became known as the Trail of Tears.

Since there were now more of these newcomers than the older groups in Oklahoma Territory, Ross was elected chief of the entire group and held that position until his death in 1866. He was an excellent leader who furthered law, education, and religion among all Cherokees.

Some 500 Eastern Cherokees escaped to the Smoky Mountains during the evacuation. There they lived as illegal refugees for many years, barely surviving on the sparse vegetation and animal life of the area. A few hundred other Cherokees were exempted from the forced evacuation and remained in North Carolina. These and a few returning tribesmen made up the ancestors of today's Eastern band.

In 1805, a white child, William Thomas, was born near Waynesville, North Carolina. His father died shortly before he was born, and the boy grew up an orphan. By the time he was twelve, he was working in an Indian trading post owned by a local lawyer and congressman's family. Shortly after he started to work in the store, Will was noticed by the nearby chief, who adopted him into his own family. Will was bright and quickly learned to speak and write the Cherokee language. He furthered his education greatly when the store failed and the owner paid Will in law books.

The old chief was one of those left by the Trail of Tears in 1838. He groomed young Will for leadership of the tribe, and when he died in 1843, recommended that the Indians around him get Will to lead them. Will, understanding all their problems, was glad to do so. He, being white, could legally buy land for them, which he did as long as he lived. This adopted Cherokee became a United States senator later on and was responsible for a law recognizing them as citizens.

The eastern tribesmen became a peaceful and fairly prosperous group again. And after debts had been cleared up, the section helped by Will Thomas, with good lawyers working for them, became today's reservation, the Qualla Boundary, in 1876. Under much friendlier conditions with whites, they were then chartered by the state of North Carolina in 1889.

Cherokee, North Carolina, is their capital, just as Tahlequah is the capital of the Western band in Oklahoma. They do not live in a densely populated area, but are scattered all along rural roads near Cherokee. From 6,000 to 7,000 live on the reservation. Of course, today they dress, look and act like other Americans (except for those in the Oconaluftee Indian Village on the edge of the town).

A federal agency for them is located in Cherokee. The agency gives technical advice of all kinds to them. The federal government provides health care, hospitals, dentists, and doctors. One high school and several grade schools are furnished, but the children can also attend the regular public schools if they wish. Only the oldest ones speak Cherokee, though attempts are still being made to preserve their language and culture (by the Cherokee Historical Association).

This organization also sponsors the Oconaluftee Indian Village, which presents an excellent picture of Cherokee life 200 years ago. It is open from May 15 through October 25 each year. It is well worth your time to see this "village" if you visit the Smoky Mountains.

Likewise, you should not miss the wonderful outdoor drama "Unto These Hills" which has been presented each night except Sunday for the last forty-five years. The drama is presented at a mountainside theater, and perhaps is the most popular outdoor play in the United States. It tells their story from the arrival of De Soto in 1540 until the Trail of Tears, with Andy Jackson and Sequoyah playing important roles, and the spectacular Eagle Dances being performed each night.

The Eastern band owns and operates an excellent museum in the town of Cherokee. Open year round, the museum presents videotapes, artifacts, native crafts, and a movie of their historic development. Special "hear phones" allow one to hear the syllabary of Sequoyah. Some of the old myths and legends are presented in colorful stained acrylic windows. Visitors leave this bit of the past understanding better the tragic history of these people. Authentic arts and crafts are sold in the gift shop and in the Qualla shop across the street.

The Smoky Mountain area of the Cherokee Reservation is so beautiful, it is not surprising that the Eastern band did not want to leave for western lands.

The Cherokee Alphabet

D$_a$	R$_e$	T$_i$	δ_o	O$_u$	i$_v$
S$_{ga}$ O$_{ka}$	F$_{ge}$	y$_{gi}$	A$_{gv}$	J$_{gu}$	E$_{gv}$
θ_{ha}	P$_{he}$	ϑ_{hi}	F$_{ho}$	Γ_{hu}	Φ_{hv}
W$_{la}$	ℓ_{le}	P$_{li}$	G$_{lo}$	M$_{lu}$	ϑ_{lv}
δ_{ma}	O$_{me}$	H$_{mi}$	5_{mo}	y$_{mu}$	
θ_{na} t$_{hna}$ G$_{nah}$	Λ_{ne}	h$_{ni}$	Z$_{no}$	ϑ_{nu}	O$_{nv}$
$\mathbb{T}_{qua}$	ω_{que}	P$_{qui}$	V$_{quo}$	ω_{quu}	$\mathcal{E}_{quv}$
U$_{sa}$ ω_s	4_{se}	b$_{si}$	$\mp_{so}$	$\mathcal{E}_{su}$	R$_{sv}$
L$_{da}$ W$_{ta}$	S$_{de}$ T$_{te}$	J$_{di}$ J$_{ti}$	Λ_{dv}	S$_{du}$	Γ_{dv}
δ_{dla} L$_{tla}$	L$_{tle}$	C$_{tli}$	ϑ_{tlo}	ϑ_{tlu}	P$_{tlv}$
G$_{tsa}$	V$_{tse}$	h$_{tsi}$	K$_{tso}$	J$_{tsu}$	C$_{tsv}$
G$_{wa}$	ω_{we}	O$_{wi}$	O$_{wo}$	ϑ_{wu}	6$_{wv}$
ω_{ya}	B$_{ye}$	ϑ_{yi}	6$_{yo}$	G$_{yu}$	B$_{yv}$

94

Glossary

Anglo: North Americans who speak English, and whose culture came from an English-speaking country.

aristocratic: upper class, sometimes snobbish.

brave: old Indian word for warrior.

carnage: massacre brought about by war.

Colonneh: Cherokee word for raven (Sam Houston was given this name).

dialect: the variety of language used in a certain area, or by a certain group.

etching: burning (with acid) or engraving images on metal.

evacuation: to leave a threatened area.

expedition: a journey or trip for a special purpose.

exposure: being unprotected from light or weather.

Green Corn Dance: Cherokee festival to celebrate harvest of corn, and preparation for new year.

"homing instinct": ability to find way home.

interpreting: changing from one language to another, or reading meaning into a message.

Lost Mines: legendary silver or gold mines that explorers sometimes looked for.

manhood rite: ceremony held for a boy when he became a "man," usually at the age of twelve.

medallion: an ornament to wear around the neck.

outlandish: bizarre; unfamiliar.

pension: a sum of money paid after a person works a number of years and retires.

Phoenix: legendary bird who rose from ashes; also name of first Cherokee paper.

secession: getting out of a union, as Confederate states seceded from United States before the Civil War.

smithy: nickname for blacksmith.

"squatters' rights": rights to land after living on it a certain length of time, usually five years.

stickball: contact sport played with sticks, something like skateless hockey.

syllabary: phonetic written language of Cherokee, not of letters but of sounds.

"talking leaves": what Seqouyah called written pages.

tunic and turban: wrap-around cap and long blouse worn by Cherokees in early 1800s.

Bibliography

Bealer, Alexander W. *Only the Name Remains the Same.* Boston: Little, Brown and Company, 1972.

Canfield, Leon H. and Wilder, Howard B. *The Making of Modern America.* Boston: Houghton Mifflin Company, 1956.

Carpenter, Allan. *Sam Houston, Champion of America.* Vero Beach, FL: Rourke Publishers, 1987.

Catlin, George. *Letters and Notes on North American Indians.* NY: Potter Publishers, 1975.

Connor, Seymour V. and Pool, William. *Texas, the 28th Star.* Austin-Dallas: Graphic Ideas, 1972.

Clark, Electa. *Cherokee Chief, Life of John Ross.* NY: MacMillan Company, 1970.

Crawford, Ann F. *Sam Houston, American Hero.* Austin: Eakin Press, 1988.

Cushman, Ralph B. *Jesse Chisholm.* Austin: Eakin Press, 1992.

Cwiklik, Robert. *Sequoyah and the Cherokee Alphabet.* Englewood Cliffs, NJ: Silver Burdett Press, 1989.

Ehli, John. *The Trail of Tears.* NY: Doubleday, 1988.

Ellis, Jerry. *Walking the Trail.* NY: Delacorte, 1991.

Flanigan, Sue. *Trailing the Longhorns.* Austin: Madrona Press, 1974.

Francis, M. E. *Jim Bowie's Lost Mine.* San Antonio: Naylor Company, 1954.

Fritz, Jean. *Make Way for Sam Houston.* NY: Putnam's, 1986.

Gard, Wayne. *Chisholm Trail.* Norman, OK: University of Oklahoma Press, 1954.

Graff, Henry F. and Kraut, John. *The Advancement of the American People.* Chicago: Rand McNally, 1973.

Gregg, Josiah. *Commerce of the Prairies.* NY: Bobbs Merrill Company, 1970.

Gregory, Jack, and Strickland, Rennard. *Sam Houston with the Cherokees.* Austin: University of Texas, 1967.

Haley, James L. *An Album of American History.* NY: Doubleday, 1985.

Handbook of Texas. Austin: Texas: State Historical Association, 1952.

Irving, Washington. *A Tour of the Prairies.* NY: Pantheon Books, 1967.

James, Marquis. "The Run for the Cherokee Strip," *Advancement in American Literature.* NY: Harcourt, 1958.

Kehoe, Alice. *North American Indians.* Englewood Cliffs, NJ: Prentice-Hall.

Kephart, Horace. *Our Southern Highlands.* Knoxville, TN: University of Tennessee, 1976 (Introduction by George Ellison).

Latham, Lee. *Sam Houston, Hero of Texas.* NY: Chelsea House, 1991.

Lepthian, Emilie. *The Cherokee.* Chicago: Children's Press, 1985.

Marriot, Alice. *Sequoyah, Leader of the Cherokee.* NY: Random House, 1956.

McReynolds, ———. *Oklahoma, A History of the Sooner State.* Norman, OK: Univeristy of Oklahoma, 1954.

McCall, Barbara A. *The Cherokee.* Vero Beach, FL: Rouke Publishing, Co., 1989.

Mooney, James. *James Mooney's History, Myths, and Sacred Formulas of the Cherokees.* Ashville, NC: Historical Images, 1992.

Montgomery, Mosier, and Bethel. *The Growth of Oklahoma,* 1933.

Perdue, Theda. *Cherokee.* NY: Chelsea, 1989.

Pearson, Jim; Proctor, Ben; and Conroy, William. *Texas, Its Lands and Its People:* Dallas: Hendrick-Long, 1987.

Sharp, J. Ed. *The Cherokees, Past and Present.* Cherokee, NC: Cherokee Publications, 1970.

Stein, R. Conrad. *The Story of the Trail of Tears.* Chicago: Children's Press, 1985.

98

Taylor, T. U. *Jesse Chisholm.* Bandera, TX: Frontier Times, 1939.

Tinkle, Lon. *13 Days to Glory.* NY: McGraw Hill, 1958.

Tinkle, Lon. *An American Original.* Boston: Little, Brown, and Company, 1978.

Underwood, Tom B. *The Story of the Cherokee People.* Cherokee, NC: Cherokee Publications, 1961.

Ward, Ralph T. *Steamboats.* NY: Bobbs Merrill Company, 1956.

Worcester, Don. *The Chisholm Trail.* Lincoln, NE: University of Nebraska Press, 1981.

Encyclopedias:
Encyclopedia Americana. Danberry, CT: Grolier Inc., 1989.
The World Book Encyclopedia. Chicago: World Book, Inc., 1993.

Pamphlets:
The Indian Texans. San Antonio: Institute of Texan Cultures, 1970.

"Museum of Cherokee Indians." Cherokee, NC: Cherokee Publishers, 1994.

"Oconoluftee Indian Village." Cherokee, NC: Southern Highlands Attractions, 1994.

"Qualla Arts and Crafts Museum," (catalog). Cherokee, NC: 1994.

"Unto These Hills," Drama of the Cherokee (program). Cherokee, NC: 1994.

Miscellaneous:
American Indians, Culture in Conflict. Senior Scholastic, NY: October 13, 1989.

Mary Chiltowsky to Sybil O'Rear (letter) May 12, 1994.

"A Time for Going Back." Judy Johnston, *The Cherokee One Feather,* Wednesday, May 25, 1994.

"Report to the People (from principal chief), *The Cherokee One Feather,* September 14, 1994.

Source Guide and Class Notes from George Ellison, Elder Hostel Session, Highlands Mountain, GA, September 1994.

— Courtesy the artist, Russell Cushman